Rat and Cat

in

The Hat!

Written by
Jeanne Willis

Illustrated by
Gabriele Antonini

Rat was in bed.
"Got you!" said Cat.

"Let me go!" said Rat.

Cat let Rat go.
Rat got a hat.

"What is in the hat?" said Cat.

"A bat!" said Rat.

Rat got into the hat.

"Rat is in the hat!" said Cat.

Rat was not in the hat.
It was a can of nuts!

Rat was in the can!
Rat ran off.

"You can not get me!"
said Rat.

"Yes I can!"
said Cat.